How to Thrive in the Planning Jungle

100 Tips for Consultants, Real Estate Developers and Architects

Lorenzo Pandolfi

ISBN: 978-1-0369-0002-1

Table of Contents

Foreword

by James Maurici KC, Landmark Chambers

In the summer of 2024, Lorenzo emailed me with a preview of this book.

He wrote modestly that "If it is a damp squib, I'd rather extinguish it now." But it was no damp squib! I absolutely loved what I read. The writing style is concise and crisp. The book is full of wisdom as well as humour.

The title *How to Thrive in the Planning Jungle* is certainly apt. As Lorenzo says, "The jungle is muddy, full of traps and strange creatures."

I would add that the OED Online contains this definition of the word "jungle" when used figuratively *"A wild, tangled mass. Also, a place of bewildering complexity or confusion; a place where the 'law of the jungle' prevails; a scene of ruthless competition, struggle, or exploitation…"* Well that certainly seems to encapsulate modern planning!

The OED Online goes on to quote from T. Carlyle, *Latter-day Pamphlets iii* (1850) "What a world-wide jungle of red tape." That too seems peculiarly relevant.

In a jungle, one needs a trusted guide, and Lorenzo, through this book, provides this.

It has useful tips for everyone. Not just those early in their careers but also those professionals who have been somewhat hardened by years of exploration.

Lorenzo and I share common Italian roots. There is a joy in seeing people explore beyond predetermined barriers, be it language, job title or legal systems.

I hope, and trust, that this is the first of many, many editions of the book.

Introduction

In the summer of 2014, I started cycling up and down the hills of Brighton to check the size of rear extensions, listen to angry neighbours, and talk to agitated homeowners whose project's approval or refusal ultimately depended on my personal judgement.

It was a crash course on the English town planning system and interpersonal skills.

I loved every minute of it.

At university, I learnt about the mythical New Towns and the Garden Cities idyll.

I grew fond of the British system's transparency and fair play, as opposed to the Mediterranean taste for loud debates, opaque accountability, and the occasional *sprezzatura* of building codes.

However, in my first week as an assistant planning officer, I quickly discovered that in the jungle of development control meek subscribers to Dogs Today can become werewolves if a neighbour asks permission for a conservatory two hundred meters away from their garden.

The paradise of democracy looked much fiercer than I thought when I was a student in Venice.

I later discovered that planning committee meetings can bear a striking resemblance to gladiator battles and that people occasionally build castles without planning permission and hide them behind straw bales.

Tutto il mondo è paese.

Like many other overseas graduates with limited prospects for career advancement in their home countries, I moved to England with the simple hope of finding a job in the discipline I loved.

For a few months, I shared a room with a friend in an unsavoury patch of North London.

I juggled late shifts as a waiter and the early morning bombardment of potential employers with CVs saying something like, *I have decent grades. I can adapt. Please give me a chance.*

The chance finally came when I was on the cusp of giving up, flying back to Italy, and trying a different career path, maybe as an archivist or as a farmer.

It was a rainy morning in June when everything came together in Hove. I managed to scrape through an interview with the local city council.

While committing to a healthy diet of GPDO, NPPF, and other strange names, I rapidly realised that to adapt to this new work environment, mental flexibility was essential.

Listening, analysing, and interpreting the priorities of different stakeholders was as important as knowing the difference between two separate land-use classifications.

After my first ten years in the job, I came to think that the human side of planning practice has an edge over the technical one.

You can always consult excellent books if you are in doubt about the meaning of *curtilage* (we will forever be).

However, there are not many resources available to help you manage emotions during difficult calls with angry clients or citizens or to make sound decisions under pressure.

These frictions happen in any situation where someone (the applicant) presents a real estate project to a public body with the political and legal authority to approve or deny it.

Managing the relationship between the applicant's desires and the granter's regulations is the daily work of planning officers, consultants, lawyers, or anyone who ventures into the bureaucratic morass where the future shape of our cities is determined.

No political reform will ever transform it into a garden with a perpetual summer breeze and cute kittens smiling at your project.

The jungle is muddy, full of traps and strange creatures.

The temperature is always high because town and country planning is the arena where people with very different priorities *negotiate for the control of space* (room, building, neighbourhood, city, planet).

It may be a regimented battle, but it is still a battle.

For this reason, facilitating the relationship between the negotiating parties will always be a priority to improve the system and make the exchanges less painful.

My hope is that this collection of tips will help the inhabitants and occasional explorers of the planning jungle thrive in it, or at least get out of it unscathed.

Who is this book for?

I wrote this book with real estate professionals in the early and middle stages of their careers in mind, but I hope that any insight from these pages can also benefit more seasoned players.

I have collected ideas and insights while working within the English town planning system, and it transpires in the text. However, many teachings I have learned along the way have a wider application and can be handy in any negotiation relating to a real estate project.

While this work is primarily intended for those who work in this industry, the wider general public can also find it valuable.

The principles of communication, negotiation, and understanding diverse priorities can be applied to many aspects of life beyond town planning.

When AI finally takes over and decides the fate of your new garden room instead of planning officers or zones land for future development instead of politicians, you may be tempted to chuck this book in the bin.

Even in that scenario, I would save it for tip number 100, as it might still be helpful in a Mad Max world where robotic planners rule.

Buona avventura.

Part 1: Strategy

Chapter 1:

Mindset

1: We Are Explorers

Successful real estate developers see value where others do not, before others do, or both.

They analyse largely public data to draw unique conclusions.

As consultants, we must facilitate this creative journey through space and time, venturing where others have not ventured yet or spotting new trends unnoticed by others.

Our work adds value by identifying levers that expand possibilities while respecting policy boundaries.

Go beyond the beaten path. Test the site's parameters and its nuances. Shed light on ingenious combinations of land uses.

Explore.

2: Expand Your Perspective

Clients hire you only to solve their problems, ideally with solutions that others cannot see.

Innovation always starts with a deep understanding of the basics. There is no point in attempting acrobatics if you do not know how to do simple movements.

Still, great solutions for complex projects require navigating between different policies, political pressures, and physical constraints to reach a vantage point of observation where you can identify various options that lead to the desired result. At least, you should be able to find several convenient exit routes if things go wrong.

Your client requires a refined perspective that clearly maps both the paths to victory and the least painful paths to an elegant retreat.

Make all the necessary moves to reach that viewing platform of top-quality advice.

The opposite is also valid. Do not perform a somersault when a simple step (forward, back, or sideways) would suffice. There is no need to climb a mountain when the battle can be won on flat ground.

And sometimes, the best acrobats feign clumsiness to wow the audience later on.

3: Anticipate Scrutiny

When you think about an issue or when you are about to write a paragraph to defend an element of a project, always imagine having a top-class, ruthless, and witty barrister on the opposite side testing your arguments with razor-sharp precision.

This imaginary adversary should not frighten you. Just keep it at the back of your mind.

If you think that your arguments are based on solid technical evidence, a balanced planning judgement, and fair advocacy on behalf of your client's interests, go ahead and write.

If you think that the arguments are shaky, be honest with yourself and think again about how to resolve the issue.

This mental opponent will keep questioning you until you ensnare it within a robust framework of analysis and argumentation.

4: Do Not Hide

In most projects, there are elements that comply with planning policy and others that do not.

This is the very essence of planning consultancy: building a case in favour of the client by putting all pros and cons on the planning balance.

The key is to *always* address *all* the planning policy considerations of relevance for the case at hand, from the most important ones to the (apparently) minor ones, from the ones that are clearly in line with policy and can boost your chances of success to those that are obviously contrary to policy and can lead to a refusal.

List them all. Assess them all.

When there is something that works against you, analyse it and try to resolve it. If it is not resolvable, explain why, after all, the planning balance is still in favour of a "yes."

Never sweep under the carpet evidence or planning policies that work against you. Tackle them head-on.

5: Firmness and Flexibility

In negotiations and dealings with stakeholders and partners, you should be firm and flexible at the same time.

While this may be challenging, it can help you navigate through challenging situations. The ability to strike a balance between these two seemingly contradictory qualities is critical in planning and real estate, where the needs of different parties frequently clash.

Firmness involves standing your ground on key principles. As a professional, you are often the gatekeeper of rules that ensure fairness and safety. You need to understand when and where to draw the line, especially in situations where compromising could have negative consequences in the long run.

Flexibility is about knowing when to bend without breaking. The planning system is inherently complex, and every project presents unique challenges and opportunities. Adapting to these nuances is often essential for achieving a positive outcome. Flexibility should never compromise your core values, though.

The key to combining the two is adaptability. Adaptable professionals are not tied to a single way of thinking or predetermined plan. They are reactive enough to assess situations as they unfold and modify their strategies to align with the current reality.

6: Laser-Focused Analysis

The brilliance of a chef is not as important as the quality of the ingredients.

Even Michelin-starred restaurants cannot serve a dish if their eggs are rotten.

The success of any real estate project is primarily determined by meticulous analysis.

The core elements for the crafting of a powerful planning case are the X-rays of planning policies, the characteristics of the site, and the added value that the project can bring to the area.

If you lose focus on the project's progress and your client's goals, go back to the core ingredients.

When you find yourself immersed in the intricate preparation of a challenging recipe, where the input of multiple chefs can significantly influence the result, remember the fundamentals.

Analyse the most important elements in order of importance (substance), leaving the antics of presentation (form) for a later moment.

When you have too much on your plate, find a quiet corner and start by chopping humble onions with focus and intent. Then, proceed to sauces. Afterwards, go back to the complex recipe again.

This approach will clarify the components of the whole, ensuring the dish is the best it can be when it leaves the kitchen.

7: United Front

There is nothing worse than showing the other party involved in a negotiation that there are internal discrepancies within your team.

Differences in opinion are normal among two or more individuals, and this is particularly true in large teams of expert professionals.

However, you cannot have a productive discussion with other stakeholders without a set of fixed internal parameters.

If you cannot show that you are a unified body with a clear line of action rather than a collection of people with slightly different perspectives, you will start off on the wrong foot.

Smooth out differences internally as much as possible. If reasonable alternative options or diverging opinions cannot be synthesised in a single set of arguments, decide which options and/or opinions should be presented first and which ones should be either used later or mentioned only if the other options fail.

The same applies to your exchanges of ideas with your end client. The client always has the final say, but it is your duty to ensure that all the voices are heard at the right time before the orchestra (the project team) goes on stage to perform the agreed score.

8: Simple Communications

Verbosity is often a sign of arrogance or lack of clarity. Or both.

Succinct verbal and written communication ensures that your points get across quicker so they can be interpreted quicker.

Using plain English ensures that anyone reading your report can relate to it without feeling left out.

It does not mean that they will agree with you, but at least you will not have to fight against your own pomposity. In relation to communications with the project team and your client, always retain a form of professional detachment and avoid colloquial language.

Ensure that your emails are concise and clear. Nine times out of ten, an email with a well-structured list of bullet points is more effective than a lengthy one.

On the tenth occasion, you should provide more context and analysis. Even then, it would probably be better to put the longer explanation in a separate note and only keep the essential points in the email.

9: Operation Janus

To leap ahead of competitors in the future, delve deeply into the past.

The political management of space is not a science. Innovation in this discipline is limited.

Since our ancestors fought over patches of grass where to plant a tent, the topic of drawing lines (imaginary or real) on the face of the earth has stirred up a lot of emotions.

The control of space evokes primordial instincts, which are luckily now regimented into a democratic system that is ruled by law. Despite this, the instincts linger on.

Therefore, it is crucial to strive for a deep understanding of human nature, incorporating it into your training. As a result, you will become a more proficient operator in the field of town planning, which serves as the foundation for negotiating human priorities for the use of space.

Explore what is inside the black box that makes the world move.

Try to understand the basics of social science, psychology, and ways to embrace different worldviews.

Ideally, you should feel equally comfortable in a shoddy, unauthorised suburban garden shed and in the halls of a Grade I-listed palace. Try to grasp the reason why they both exist and why they generate different reactions from end users, citizens, and politicians.

This mental flexibility will make you a better advisor when it comes to changing the shape of the world, as you will be able to better comprehend the rules that influence the behaviour of its inhabitants.

10: Cherish Crises

Managing a crisis successfully is a hundred times more rewarding than simply sailing through normal waters.

Avoiding a crisis is crucial, but if you have the ability to resolve it or at least lessen its impact, you will emerge as a hero for both your team and your client.

So, try to use your tactical and technical skills. Reduce the pressure in the room (or in the email chain). Be perceived as the person who either resolves the crisis or makes it less painful for all.

Even if the crisis is not fully resolved and the outcome is negative, you will have glued together your fellow travellers, reinforcing your bond for any future difficulties.

When you give your absolute best, you win even if you lose.

11: Never Forget That Planning, at Its Core, Is Politics

Planning, a direct offspring of politics, is one of its most unruly children.

Even the driest space standard or innocuous policy on the acceptable size of rear extension is a tool devised, systemised, and enforced by professionals who have an explicit or implicit political mandate.

Successfully bringing a project to fruition always necessitates strategic interaction with local authorities, ranging from brief conversations with junior planning officers to well-structured presentations to town councillors.

Success often depends on understanding the political landscape and aligning your project with the local needs. Other times, it depends on making sure that your project resolves important issues at a high level, thus justifying any localised collateral damage.

Even in that scenario, the final decision will be made on the basis of politics-soaked documents, so always try to understand what makes politicians tick.

Chapter 2:

The Project

12: Amplify Positive Effects

The size of a project does not determine its magnitude.

Even small changes to the complexion of a city can trigger big benefits. Find a way to create space for your project to shine, and make sure that the project's consumers understand the value you have added.

A single small violin can dominate an empty room if there are no other conflicting sounds overpowering it. You do not need amplifiers in that situation. A single small building can enliven the face of a street.

The key is to identify the small yet powerful elements of your project that can bring out the best in its environment. These details seem minor, but they can create ripples of positive change that extend far beyond the project's immediate footprint.

13: Resolve Local Issues, Even if Local Stakeholders Do Not Want to Resolve Them

Understanding the problems that affect a particular area of a city is the first step to using them to your advantage.

Sometimes, local residents and politicians are interested in resolving these issues. Sometimes, they are not.

Try to always clearly contribute to an improvement or even the complete resolution of the issue. When you do something that is measurably good, above and beyond local interests, you will have set the bar for refusal much higher.

If your request for project approval is refused, the decision maker(s) on the upper echelons of the decision-making hierarchy—which are usually independent and impartial—will notice your effort, in spite of local opposition or apathy.

Imagine an old house with hardwood floors hidden beneath a tired, dusty carpet. The carpet has been there for years. People have grown accustomed to its presence. They have stopped questioning what might lie underneath. Some might resist removing it, fearing the effort or problems it might reveal.

Lift that carpet, see what is below, and try to clean it.

14: Expand the Outreach of Your Project

A good building goes beyond the basics of providing shelter for human activities within a well-designed envelope.

It triggers emotions and a sense of belonging.

I have never visited the Taj Mahal, but its underlying message has reached me several times through the media. If its architects and builders had proposed a new project in my area, I would have subconsciously considered it as an honour rather than a nuisance.

Try to appeal to the different sensibilities of people living in the area and humans in general. Try to expand the effect of your project beyond the basics of aesthetics and functionality.

If you appeal to various groups, you will have a better chance of mustering support, and you will remain in their hearts once the project is completed.

At the next round, you will stand out from the crowd, having completed numerous popular projects.

15: Raise the Political Stakes

You must navigate the political landscape before you can raise the stakes.

Know who the key players are—local councillors, community leaders, and influential residents. Understand their motivations and how your project fits into the political dynamics.

Is there an upcoming election? Are there local issues your project could address?

Position your effort as a crucial piece in a larger political puzzle. For example, if the local government is pushing for economic growth, emphasise how your development will create jobs and boost revenue. This will make it politically advantageous for decision-makers to support you.

Engage the public and media to amplify your message. A well-orchestrated public relations campaign can turn your project into a community cause, making it harder for decision-makers to oppose it.

Make your moves meaningful, and always try to enter the local political discourse with frankness and clarity.

16: Think Big, Even in Small Projects

Thinking big is not just for large developments; it is a mindset that can transform modest initiatives into something far greater.

A small project can be like a single ingredient in a recipe. It might seem insignificant on its own, but with the right vision, it can elevate the entire dish.

As a pinch of the right spice can transform a meal, a well-conceived small project can enhance the character of a neighbourhood or even set a new standard for future developments.

Remember that each project can accomplish more than it appears. Small projects offer opportunities for innovation that might be more challenging in larger developments.

They are opportunities to make your creativity shine and prove that small, thoughtful touches can make a big difference.

17: Give Assists Instead of Scoring Goals

We are educated to prefer prominence to obscurity. We all want to be Mbappé, Michael Jordan, or Messi. However, when refining and negotiating a real estate project (internally or externally), it is often better to give assists than score.

Collaboration is crucial during the process of developing and negotiating a project. When you give an assist, you empower others to shine, which reinforces the teamwork spirit. This strengthens relationships and builds goodwill. The ability to work well with others can be just as important as your individual contributions.

Like a playmaker on the field, your role is to set others up for success, which in turn drives the project forward. This applies to both members of your team and counterparts.

Also, if you let other scores, they will remember your assist forever. They will return the favour whenever possible. At worst, they will know that it is rewarding to play with you and will be happy to see your face again.

18: Translate Commercial Objectives Into Public Benefits

We often find ourselves performing a translator role—interpreting and balancing the languages of profitability and public interest.

Our job is to take the raw, economically-driven objectives of property developers and reframe them into something that aligns with policies, values, and political goals.

Property developers speak the language of return on investment, market demand, and financial viability. Politicians, planners, and the public speak in terms of community welfare, environmental sustainability, and long-term social impact. Bridging these two worlds requires an understanding of the underlying needs of both parties.

Skilled translators do not just convert words; they capture the essence of meaning.

Similarly, a planner must reframe commercial objectives to fit within the public planning framework. This means reshaping proposals so that they deliver tangible communal benefits while still meeting the developer's financial goals.

Making numbers stack up and benefiting the public at large is a difficult sweet spot to find, but that spot is where genuinely sustainable development is created.

19: Add Salt Gradually

Salt can be added to but not taken away from a dish.

When possible, start with no salt at all and add it as needed. If you add too much or too quickly, the project may become unpalatable. If the project's ingredients are really good, you do not need to add enhancers at all.

The job of planning consultants (and real estate consultants in general) is to secure every possible advantage for your client as quickly as possible.

However, starting with an overly ambitious proposal can lead to unnecessary push-backs. It is better to introduce elements slowly and adjust the recipe based on feedback.

20: Do Not Be Fixed; Move With the Flow

Good architects design solutions, not buildings.

Average architects remain focused on their projects as initially conceived. They are aghast when team members propose changes.

Good architects are listening to the needs of the client, the ideas of collaborators, and the faint voice of the *genius loci*. Then, and only then, they start incorporating these factors into a project.

The best ones shun rigidity. Rigidity is the main characteristic of buildings, which are the *end* product of the design process.

The initial phases of exploration are fluid by necessity. Curveballs are opportunities to reshape thinking, not resist it.

Stiffness imposed too early kills innovation. Moving with the flow allows for ideas to evolve, which leads to solutions that work harmoniously with all factors at play.

Try to embrace the curve balls and allow them to contribute to the final shape of the project.

This will help you embed adaptability in the project team's discussions.

21: Identify Immediately the Pawns That Can Be Lost

Every real estate project has aspects that hold great value and others that, while seemingly important, can be sacrificed.

A skilled chess player knows which pawns to protect and which they can lose without jeopardising the strategy. The same is true in town planning. You must be able to identify the elements of your project that can be negotiated or discarded early on.

Project teams often try to defend every detail, causing unnecessary friction with stakeholders. Determine which parts of your project are non-essential and be ready to sacrifice them.

By proactively offering up these "pawns," you demonstrate flexibility. The move creates a sense of goodwill with the decision-makers. You protect the integrity of what truly matters, steering the project toward a smoother approval process.

Keep the larger picture in mind. Do not be afraid to let go of a few details to secure the bigger win.

22: Avoid the Word "Unique"

No two buildings are the same, yet they all serve the same purpose.

Calling every project "unique" is a common mistake. We often use the term as a hollow buzzword to elevate the ordinary. Very few projects are truly one-of-a-kind. Leaning too heavily on this label could risk diluting the true value of your work.

A project should be set apart because of its substance—the thoughtful planning, intelligent design, the ways it responds to its environment, and the tangible benefits it brings to the community.

Every building or project has to strike a balance between fitting into its context and enhancing it. A well-designed project does not need the crutch of being labelled as "unique." It should speak for itself.

Avoid trite soundbites and focus on the mettle of your design.

Chapter 3:

Negotiations

23: Be Patient

Patience is not just a virtue; it is a strategic asset.

Negotiations are often drawn-out processes that involve multiple stakeholders with diverse interests, so achieving consensus takes time. Rushing through negotiations can lead to suboptimal outcomes and missed opportunities.

Being patient allows the other side to express their needs without pressure, which builds trust and provides valuable insights.

Being patient also means knowing when to push forward and when to hold back, as not every moment is right for making demands or closing deals.

Stepping back and giving the process a moment to breathe can allow emotions to settle, positions to clarify, and new information to emerge that might shift the dynamics of the negotiation.

Try to understand the *rhythm* of the negotiation process and follow it.

24: Be Assertive

Assertiveness means confidently expressing your needs, desires, and boundaries without being dismissive of others.

It is a balance between standing your ground and remaining open to change positions.

When practised effectively, assertiveness helps ensure that your voice is heard and your interests are advocated for.

Communicate your points firmly but with empathy. State your position without hesitation or ambiguity, then be prepared to negotiate from a place of confidence. Assertive communicators are clearly focused on their goals.

Assertiveness helps prevent misunderstandings and reduces the likelihood of using wrong assumptions. By addressing issues directly, you can find solutions that satisfy both parties' needs.

Do not mistake it for aggression. Avoid confrontational behaviour, which can alienate others and hinder progress. On the other hand, being passive or overly accommodating can undermine your position. Communicate your needs and boundaries effectively.

Assertiveness could lead to push-back, so be ready to handle resistance professionally and use it as an opportunity to negotiate further.

25: Be Sensible

Ambition is crucial for success, but never at the expense of practicality.

Sensibility is the capacity to make decisions based on reality while pursuing your goals with tenacity.

You have to understand the context and constraints within which you are negotiating. It requires a realistic assessment of what is achievable and what is not, followed by choices that align with these assessments.

Being sensible does not mean being overly accommodating; you should continue to pursue your objectives but do so with a realistic and grounded approach, acknowledging and working within the boundaries of the possible.

26: Defuse the Situation

When a room is too hot, opening a window is the simplest and most effective way to refresh the air.

You do not need complicated air conditioning, which may or may not work. Just a simple turn of the window knob will do.

The same applies to difficult conversation, on whichever platform the conversation is taking place.

Never swallow the bait of innuendo.

At one end of the spectrum (aggression), the best reaction to a gigantic barking dog is to stand still. On the other end (passive aggression), the best reaction to a dose of poison is to increase the proportion of water in the mix, giving more space and time to the attacker to go beyond gratuitous frustration and get to the point that we all want to resolve.

Either way, always be the one lowering the temperature in the room. When the climate is more amicable, things get sorted quicker.

27: De-Escalate

When people are angry, they tend to make things bigger or more difficult than they actually are.

Remove the hyperbole from the email/phone call/discussion you are having. Focus on the size, location, and cause of the real pain points.

Reduce the spectacular to the practical to focus on the only thing that matters: finding solutions.

Sometimes, the problems are really big, pressing, and dangerous. In that case, you should focus on the single most pressing issue that stands out from the others.

Even containing its effects temporarily would buy you time and space. It will avoid a collapse of the discussion, which is the absolute worst-case scenario. It is even worse than death (being for a business loss of money, loss of reputation, legal issues, etc.)

"Death" is part of nature, as each business sooner or later dies or evolves into something else.

The end of a dialogue is not part of nature, where different elements (including contrasting ones) perpetually interact with each other by default.

The end of a dialogue is a choice made by the parties involved in the dialogue. It cannot be tolerated in a business environment built on trust.

Always try to talk.

28: Discuss

When you have created space and time for a more detailed review of the problem at hand, isolate the key issue (or issues) that have caused it and talk to your team as soon as possible.

Timing is essential in difficult situations. Attempting to buy time by de-escalating the conflict with the other party, only to lose valuable time internally due to slow troop mobilisation, would be insane.

Time lost for your fault is lost twice.

When your team is around the table, explain the problem clearly and then discuss openly a set of possible solutions. Collaboration among team members united in the goal of solving the issue which often leads to new perspectives and unexpected ideas. When organised in an effective manner, these can result in a powerful solution.

Do not hold onto the room or email pressure. Divide it into manageable topics, and then ask your wider team to assist you.

29: Determine

It is irrelevant whether a single person, a group of people, or a democratic vote determines the appropriate response to an emergency.

What matters is that there is *one* course of action, and the whole team backs it up as one individual.

When you go back to the counterpart to find a way out for both, unity is essential.

A course of action can include several smaller actions. Some of them may vary or be replaced when the discussion resumes. This is not an issue, as flexibility is another essential quality of a good negotiator. The issue emerges when the team fails to reach a consensus internally regarding the plan of action.

The end point must be agreed; how you get there is secondary. If a new end point becomes available or if the agreed end point is no longer reachable, it is time to talk again.

Never shake hands on something that you have not charted before the trip. Maps are the only way out of dangerous places.

30: Direct

Direct the messenger to give clear instructions to the other party. Give the person your full support to untangle the problem. As much as the situation allows, let them feel covered and comfortable. Then, be direct.

Apologies rarely work. What people want are alternative options, solutions, and ways out.

By offering alternative options, you provide variables that might even eliminate the problem entirely.

A fight over the last available pizza in a restaurant can dissolve if both guests prefer a type of salad that is on the menu even more than the pizza.

With solution(s), you give your interlocutors a range of paths to get out of the impasse, and each of them will appease them to different degrees. Ideally, one of them will clear the sky completely.

Ways out, which are one of the most refined results of negotiations, replace the unsolvable problem with a bigger benefit on a different level, reserving you even more time to resolve the main problem outside the spotlights.

The initial rage is repaid with kindness, and the elephant in the room is quietly moved to its natural habitat (or a different room) where experts of elephants can turn it more amicable.

31: If You Have Changed Position, Say It

If you alter your position on an issue or in a negotiation, communicate it clearly.

Things change. External factors may reveal new information or alter circumstances. Adaptability frequently necessitates adjusting your stance as a strategic maneuver. Failure to communicate the change can lead to mistrust.

State your change clearly and directly. Explain the reasons behind the change to help others understand the rationale and see the change as a thoughtful decision.

Be open to questions about the change, and then adjust your negotiation strategies based on the new position. Ensure that all parties have a clear understanding of how this shift will impact the negotiation.

However, always check that such changes are justified, since frequent or unwarranted spins can undermine your credibility and disrupt the negotiation process.

32: Shed Light on Topics That Can Help the Counterpart

If you have brought good food to a picnic, why would you leave it in your bag instead of sharing it?

Being generous with information that can benefit the other party can be a powerful tactic.

When you shed light on topics that can help the counterpart, you are essentially adding a sprinkle of cooperation to the negotiation table.

It can transform it from a competitive battle into a cooperative effort, where both sides are more likely to find mutually beneficial solutions.

It demonstrates your commitment to both parties' success, which tends to facilitate future negotiations.

Determine what information or insights could benefit the other party and explain why.

Choose the right moment to share information since offering insights too early or too late in the process can affect their impact.

33: Keep Your Best Cards for the Last Round, or Do Not Use Them at All

Putting forward your strongest arguments at the right moment can give you a decisive edge, so it is important to use your most valuable points or concessions tactfully.

Retaining control over the outcome is ensured by withholding your most powerful arguments or concessions until the final negotiation stages. Revealing them at the right moment will maximise their impact.

Ensure that your final offer or argument is compelling.

However, you should not rely solely on your best cards to win the game. Focus on building a strong foundation first. You may not even need to use your best cards at all.

Keep in mind that playing those cards too late can also backfire, so ensure that the timing aligns with the negotiation dynamics and the other party's readiness.

Part 2: Interpersonal Skills

Chapter 4:

The Clients

34: Present Yourself Before Presenting Solutions

With new contacts, with new clients, and in situations where you are parachuted into a project with an established team, remember that the first rule of politeness is to introduce yourself at the beginning of the conversation.

Make it clear from the start that you have all the necessary skills to contribute significantly to the project.

Begin with a summary of your role and your relevant experience. If necessary, highlight any specific expertise or qualifications that are pertinent to the project at hand. This helps demonstrate that you are a valuable addition to the team.

Try to engage with your audience. Ask about their roles and show interest in their perspectives. This builds rapport and demonstrates that you value their input.

Avoid overwhelming your audience with excessive information but provide enough detail about your experience to give a clear picture of your abilities, since being too vague can leave room for doubt about your suitability.

35: Total Commitment

Your client's interests are *your* interests.

You must prioritise client needs and then turn them into actionable steps to achieve the goal.

Your primary responsibility is to fully understand the needs through active listening and insightful questions, which you can then translate into practical steps.

Show proactive involvement by regularly updating the clients on progress, anticipating their needs, and addressing potential issues before they arise.

Total commitment involves going beyond the basic requirements. Whether it is putting in extra hours, offering additional support, or providing extra value through innovative solutions, your willingness to exceed expectations shows your dedication.

The ideas and mindset of the clients should inform your assessment of the situation. You should always have a team attitude while recognising that *they* are the ultimate directors of the team, not you.

Support and enhance their vision, not impose your own ideas or control the project.

36: Total Candour

Always choose honesty over complacency when faced with pressure, constraints, or a difficult situation.

People pay you to tell them what you *really* think.

You always have to clarify your true professional opinion on any situation the team is facing.

Even when confronted with a raging bull, you must maintain your impartiality and explain why an option is weak or is plainly wrong.

When faced with budget constraints, tight deadlines, or unforeseen challenges, the temptation to present a more convenient version of events can be strong. Total candour means resisting this urge and providing clients with your honest insights, even if uncomfortable.

However, candour does not mean that you have to forego your first duty, which is the commitment to your clients.

Unless there is a conflict of interest or a breach of professional duty, you must vigorously defend them. They always have the last word once they have heard the opinion of all of their consultants.

If you are instructed to fight, do so till the end, within the boundaries of your professional code of conduct.

37: Total Transparency

Elite chefs know how many grains of salt have been put into their dishes.

Elite planning consultants know every policy source that has been used in their reports.

When queried by clients or team members, they should be able to easily produce the list of "ingredients" of their arguments, describe why they chose them and why that particular mix of ingredients will maximise the chances of success.

Each policy, regulation, and strategy must be woven together carefully to create a compelling case. Transparency is about sharing what you're doing but also about being able to explain why every decision was made and how it serves the wider objective.

Sharing your recipe book reassures clients that every decision was carefully considered. It proves that you have nothing to hide, and each element of your approach has a clear and deliberate purpose.

Do not hide the list of ingredients; always use fresh products and avoid reheating.

38: Simple Communication, Even When Dealing With Complex Topics or Bad News

The mark of a good consultant is their ability to simplify.

A clear, straightforward message ensures that your client understands the situation and positions you as someone who can handle difficulties with professionalism.

Messages filled with jargon or too much technical detail can overwhelm clients, leaving them confused about the next steps. Clear, simple communication builds confidence and keeps everyone aligned.

Clients do not always need the full technical breakdown—they need the key points that will help them make informed decisions. Simplify the information into its essential components by focussing on what matters most.

Simplicity leads to efficiency, saving time, and keeping the focus on decision-making.

When clients understand you, they feel more confident and in control.

If you maintain complete control of communications, they will feel doubly in control of the project.

39: Boundaries…

It is important to retain personal boundaries with your clients, even the closest ones.

While building strong relationships with clients is essential to your success as a consultant, it's equally crucial to maintain a level of professional distance.

When boundaries start to blur, especially when friendships kick in, you compromise your ability to remain impartial and offer clear, balanced advice.

For a consultant, this would be like being a baker unable to bake good bread.

When you become too close to a client, the risk is that your judgement may become clouded by personal feelings or the desire to please them rather than offering objective advice. Over time, it may harm the very relationship you are trying to cultivate.

You can have a warm, cordial relationship with your client without crossing into personal territory.

If a client asks something outside the realm of your expertise or comfort, be honest about your limitations. It's not just about protecting your time and energy but also ensuring that your contributions remain valuable.

40: ...Without Borders

The point above does not imply that you should create barriers in your human relationship with your clients.

While maintaining boundaries is essential for professional impartiality, it is equally important not to create walls that prevent genuine human connection. Building rapport and engaging in meaningful conversations are vital components of a successful consultant-client relationship.

Personal connection becomes especially important in long-term projects where the relationship may extend over months or even years. In these cases, the human element helps sustain collaboration through challenging times.

Bonding creates an atmosphere of shared purpose, which in turn enhances the working relationship.

Additionally, you should be prepared to act promptly, even outside of regular business hours.

Doctors do not check their watch when duty calls, and neither should you.

You are not directly saving lives, but still, you have a direct impact on the quality of the built environment via the quality of the projects you are working on, at any time of the day.

41: Keep Them in the Loop From Day One

What clients hate most is the absence of timely communication from their consultants on the progress of a project.

It is worse than an unexpected bill or a refused permission to build. These can be justified and explained. Opaque communications patterns or radio silence cannot be.

Clients need to feel they are part of the journey, aware of every step, challenge, and victory along the way.

Establish clear communication lines as soon as you join a project. Establish clear expectations regarding the delivery of updates. If you prefer weekly reports, daily check-ins, or more ad-hoc communication based on progress, make sure the client knows this upfront.

Some clients may want highly detailed updates, while others may prefer high-level overviews. Adjust your approach to meet their expectations, but always err on the side of more frequent communication in the early stages of the project.

Maintain a steady and proportionate flow of communication—even if on certain days there is not much to report.

42: Stand by Your Professional Judgement

Never compromise on the integrity of your judgement.

Your expertise and the soundness of your professional reasoning underpin your value as a consultant. Your recommendations are informed by years of experience, education, and a thorough understanding of the intricacies of the project at hand.

The judgement may be wrong, but it is the product of your professional reasoning.

The market, the decision maker, or the law will decide if your error can stand or not the test of time.

But keep thinking, advising, and choosing your path of action solely on the basis of your inner judgement.

Own your decisions, even when faced with criticism, as long as they are born from careful analysis. Errors happen, but the strength of a professional is in the ability to stand by their choices, explain them, and adapt based on new information rather than external pressures.

Your judgement is your most valuable asset. If you allow it to be bent by external forces, you risk losing your credibility. The core of what makes you a trusted advisor will melt.

Standing firm in the face of criticism is what distinguishes great consultants from those who merely follow the path of least resistance.

This is not the same as being rigid (see above). It is about making sure your impartiality is always preserved and your standing increases as a consequence.

43: Manage Expectations With Flair

Avoid the overpromising trap.

Maintaining a healthy working relationship requires striking the right balance between what is realistically achievable and what the client hopes for.

Clients sometimes want the moon. Despite not having assembled the rocket yet, there is a temptation to assure clients that it is ready for takeoff.

However, overpromising usually leads to disappointment and a breakdown in trust. The key is to ensure that clients remain optimistic without being misled.

When you are excited about a project or when you have financial targets pressuring you from all angles, it can be tempting to paint a rosy picture.

But these risks set the team up for failure. Overpromising results in unmet deadlines, cost overruns, or failed objectives, which can sour the entire relationship well beyond a temporary loss.

To avoid the overpromising trap, , present achievable results, taking into account the project's real world limitations.

Being upfront about possible challenges sets the stage for a relationship built on trust. However, do not dampen your client's enthusiasm with a list of "what-ifs." Bolster their confidence in your ability to recognise the challenges and navigate them effectively.

44: Always Show Up

The sun shines. Birds fly. Good consultants always show up.

They are punctual and reply to emails as quickly as they can.

Reliability is one of your greatest assets. Another one is the power of being seen, heard, and *felt* (in person and virtually).

Your presence builds trust in the relationship. By always showing up, you signal that the project is a priority, and you are committed to its success. This dependability sets you apart in an industry that requires navigating complex regulations.

Clients need to know they can rely on you. Being responsive shows professionalism and respect for their time. Quick replies to messages demonstrate that you're on top of the project and addressing their concerns promptly.

Reliability is also about mental and emotional presence. Clients notice when you're fully engaged. By giving your full attention, you are recognised as someone who can always be counted on to deliver.

Chapter 5:

The Team

45: Have Fun or Go Home

Nobody is watching over your shoulder. Nobody forces you to do something. If your heart and mind are elsewhere, nobody wants you at your desk.

Freedom and inventiveness within a clear set of rules are the trademarks of elite players.

Timesheets are a hindrance.

You should try to be the best professional you can be *at all times*.

You can enrich yourself intellectually and materially while having fun along the way.

If you do not have fun, if you do not thrive in a perpetually changing gameboard, take a break or go home.

46: Explain Your Choices With Tact

It is important to maintain an atmosphere of respect when explaining decisions. Instead of presenting your choice as an absolute, frame it within the broader context of the project's goals.

Acknowledge differing opinions and emphasise that every perspective is valued, even if the final decision does not align with everyone's preferences.

If you are in charge of that particular situation, the judgement remains with you, but judges listen carefully to all the voices and carefully read all the information before settling on a specific outcome.

When a change is unpopular, clarify why you have reached the conclusion that it is the right one. Clarify why the parameters you used are not linked to personal opinions or preferences.

Lastly, pay attention to non-verbal cues, as they often indicate underlying discomfort. Address these signals promptly, offering room for questions or concerns, which demonstrates emotional intelligence and improves the working environment.

47: Be Frank

Honesty within a team is essential, but there is a fine balance between being candid and being abrasive.

When communicating with your team, it is important to be straightforward but without alienating anyone. Being frank means sharing clear, direct insights, especially when decisions need to be made quickly.

At the same time, frankness should come from a place of respect.

When delivering criticism or feedback, frame it constructively.

A good rule of thumb is to focus on the solution rather than the problem. If your team members know you are transparent but respectful, they will be more inclined to trust you and reciprocate that level of openness.

When there is an emergency, frankness also acts as an accelerator of solutions.

48: Pressure, Without Pestering

When assigning tasks, state the deadlines explicitly and leave no room for ambiguity.

Once a deadline is in sight, follow up gently but firmly.

Acknowledge the team's workload and offer support where needed but remain steadfast about the importance of the deliverables. A fruitful technique is to ask for progress updates or offer to help remove obstacles, which is in fact your only objective.

Respect the time and boundaries of your collaborators, but remind them of the urgency.

49: Unlock Positive Energy and Creativity in the Team

Encourage your team members to put their heart into their work by giving them the freedom to explore new approaches without fear of judgement. Positive reinforcement goes a long way in fuelling their creativity.

Instead of shutting down ideas that may seem unconventional, it is preferable to encourage a brainstorming session where the key players can build upon that concept.

Additionally, rotating responsibilities or pairing team members with different skills can boost morale and inspire new ways of thinking.

Encouraging open dialogue reinforces a sense of ownership and collective responsibility, and this positive energy can bring out the best ideas from every corner of the room.

Not all ingredients go well together. There is no way of mixing olive oil with water. But you need to have a space and time for free experimentation, as it bonds, refreshes, and sometimes creates excellent recipes.

The *Negroni Sbagliato* (literally the "mistaken Negroni") is one of the best cocktails out there.

50: Always Read the Company's Manuals

Although they can be a hassle, manuals are crucial to fit quickly in any organisation.

These documents are not just formalities. They contain valuable insights into the company's processes, expectations, and culture. Whether it is the employee handbook, operational guidelines, or safety protocols, these resources provide you with the basics that will inform your day-to-day actions.

Reading the manuals is the first step toward mastering the company's systems, which gives you a framework for operating within them in harmony.

By reading the company's manuals, you can avoid mistakes and reduce the time you spend asking questions that the documentation already answers.

As in a video game, you can learn the basic moves through a mix of reading and action.

You will later learn the special moves by observing top players doing them, writing down their sequence or structure, and thinking about how to use them the next time the opportunity arises.

51: Destroy the Buck of Responsibility

Great professionals do not even hold the buck. They destroy it as soon as they find it in their hands or immediately after they receive it from someone else.

You *always* have the choice to stop the blame game. You can be the solution to the problems faced by the team and the client, or at least be a key part of their solution.

As a minimum, you can always break a bucket full of fuzziness, delays, or excuses when you see it.

If a client issue or team concern comes across your desk, your goal should be to handle as much of it as you can, ensuring that everything within your power is completed.

For aspects beyond your control, pass them on to the right person with clear, actionable instructions.

Rather than imposing responsibilities on others, you build confidence within your team and with your clients by demonstrating that you're proactive.

52: Press the Reset Button

Sometimes, confusion reigns.

Half-baked information clashes with crazy deadlines, and many angry or stressed people bombard you with emails. And your boss is on holiday.

Take a deep breath and close the laptop.

Run in the park, go to the gym, shout, or sing in an empty room. Do something that is both highly energetic and liberating.

If you are collaborating with a team, consider taking them out for a coffee or a brief break as a way to relieve tension. These moments of release are crucial for resetting the atmosphere and clearing the fog.

Reset. Restart. Untangle the mess one thread at a time.

Your refreshed perspective will allow you to tackle problems more efficiently, transforming chaos into manageable steps.

Recharging is not a retreat; it is a strategy to come back stronger.

53: Clarify, Clarify, Clarify

Even if your whole library burns, keep this single principle in mind: clarity is our main goal.

Any consultant's goal is to gain the attention and understanding of as many people as possible.

To achieve this, your voice and your message should be as simple as possible.

Initially, the simplification of the message is an internal process.

You have to be clear with yourself. Then, you should translate the message into digestible morsels of information and package it into larger containers (the documents you produce). When you see a strange word or a convoluted turn of phrase, try to make it simpler.

Always assist those around you in clarifying things so that when someone points a finger, no one can hide behind jargon.

Whether you are drafting a report, crafting an email, or speaking in a meeting, cut through the fluff. Help your team strip away any unnecessary complexity.

This ensures that when the tough questions come, no one can hide behind vague language or technical terms.

54: Become a Confidant and Mediator

If you do your job well, you will naturally find yourself at the heart of many important and, at times, personal conversations.

Some of them will go beyond the remit of your consultancy. You will become an acquaintance or even a friend of colleagues, clients, and third parties.

This is an honour. It can be much more rewarding than a pay raise or a promotion. They have, in fact, promoted you to a higher league called intimacy.

Handle this responsibility with care. Your words can uplift, reassure, or redirect the team when needed.

Being a trusted confidant in confidential discussions in the changing room can sometimes shape a team's performance more than physical training under the spotlight.

55: When There Is an Emergency, Pick up the Phone

Never hide behind emails, especially when there are delicate situations, "make it or break it" bottlenecks, and unforeseen emergencies.

Faster action is needed.

Email is great for daily project management, but it often lacks the immediacy and nuance needed to resolve urgent issues.

A voice conversation allows you to quickly clarify points, gauge the tone of the other party, and reduce the potential for misinterpretation which is all too common in written communication. If a paper trail is needed, send an email after the call.

During emergencies, time is crucial. Waiting for an email reply wastes precious minutes. A phone call shows urgency, conveys your commitment, and cuts prolonged exchanges.

A personal call also makes the situation more human.

Chapter 6:

The Stakeholders

56: Zoom Out

Impulsiveness is often our number one enemy.

When you sit around a table or meet a group of stakeholders, you should zoom out to understand the background of your counterparts.

This understanding provides a more complete view of the situation. Stakeholders may be driven by factors that are not immediately visible, such as internal politics, long-standing goals, or concerns about risk.

Take time to assess the dynamics in the room, considering not just what's being said but the underlying motivation behind it. Consider also what is not being said, which has equal weight and importance.

Zooming out helps you avoid the pitfalls of reacting too quickly to surface-level information. This broader perspective can help you see where compromise is possible and identify solutions that align with everyone's interests.

When you zoom out, you not only build stronger relationships with stakeholders but also create a more constructive dialogue. You gain the trust and confidence of those around you by showing that you value their perspectives, making it easier to navigate challenges collaboratively.

57: Be Upbeat

As you interact with stakeholders, your energy can significantly impact the dynamics of the group and the progress of the project.

Being upbeat does not mean you have to be excessively cheerful or ignore real issues.

Instead, it means approaching situations with a proactive mindset. When you are upbeat, you convey confidence, which can be contagious. It helps alleviate tension and encourage a collaborative spirit among team members.

It shows that you are willing to navigate through difficulties with a positive outlook. This enhances trust and collaboration and makes stakeholders more inclined to support your initiatives.

Smiles are free. Use them freely without losing your genuineness.

58: Never Skip the Paperwork

There is no success without thorough preparation.

Preparation in the realm of real estate negotiations requires a deep dive (or more than one) into all relevant paperwork to ensure that you are fully informed and capable of making well-considered decisions.

Each document, report, and piece of correspondence holds critical information that can influence project outcomes.

Make them yourself. Find their kernel. Get them in line for use.

Try also to step above the details of the projects to analyse the processes that generated the situation you are facing.

This ensures that you are not only familiar with the current state of affairs but also aware of the historical context and underlying factors that influence the project.

Finally, study the participants of the discussion as deeply as possible before you meet them.

Read all the background information and highlight the core parameters of relevance. Review the roles of all stakeholders, their past interactions, and any specific preferences or concerns they may have.

This preparation allows you to tailor your approach to the room's atmosphere. The contents of your documents will not change, but their use will improve.

59: Never Second Guess

Decisiveness and confidence are crucial in this industry.

The act of second-guessing might seem prudent, but it can undermine your authority.

Standing by your initial judgement and expertise is crucial when faced with decisions. Second-guessing usually arises from uncertainty or the fear of making a mistake, but it can lead to indecision.

Constantly questioning your choices signals a lack of confidence to your stakeholders and team members.

Ensure that your choices are based on solid analysis. If you have done your due diligence, trust your decisions.

If new information arises or circumstances change, reassess rather than second-guess. Make adjustments as needed but avoid the trap of constantly doubting your original assumptions.

Better wrong but steady than perpetually moving between self-doubt and timidity in an attempt to be right.

60: Pre-Empt Surprises

In real estate projects, scenario planning is more important than town planning.

Start by conducting thorough risk assessments. Understand the landscape of your project and the dynamics of your stakeholders. This includes evaluating external factors that could impact on your project. Regularly update risk management plans to adapt to any new developments.

Establish contingency plans for identified risks. Having a clear plan of action for various scenarios ensures that you can respond swiftly and effectively if issues arise. This preparation helps minimise disruptions and maintain project momentum.

The goal is not to avoid surprises entirely but to be well-prepared to handle them when they occur.

By anticipating potential challenges, you can maintain control over the project and ensure a smoother path to success.

61: Never Isolate Dissenting Views—Make Them Part of a Wider Symphony

It is natural to perceive dissenting views as obstacles.

However, you can actually enhance the outcome of a project by integrating these differing perspectives into a cohesive strategy.

A single out-of-tune melody can disrupt the harmony, but when managed properly, it can also offer a unique texture that adds depth to the piece.

Similarly, we can perceive dissenting views as the "out-of-tune" elements in the project orchestra. They might seem challenging or contrary at first, but when integrated thoughtfully, they contribute to a more robust outcome.

Start by actively listening to the dissenting opinions to understand the underlying concerns.

This helps you recognise the value of these perspectives and prevents them from becoming isolated criticisms.

If you turn potential discord into harmony, you create a well-rounded project plan that resonates with all stakeholders.

62: No Prejudices

Prejudices impede our capacity to interact with stakeholders in an equitable manner, as our minds perceive obstacles that are not truly present on the field.

In project settings, prejudices can manifest as biases towards certain stakeholders based on their previous behaviour, their role, or even their background.

Any chef's task is to prepare a dish that satisfies a diverse range of tastes. If the chef lets personal biases about particular ingredients influence their cooking, they might overlook the subtleties that could make the dish exceptional.

Similarly, in project management, holding prejudices can prevent you from recognising the valuable contributions of all stakeholders, regardless of their perceived status or past actions.

Engage with any person as a valued individual rather than through the lens of past interactions or preconceived notions.

In the end, abandoning prejudices allows you to work effectively towards shared goals, ensuring that every voice contributes to the project's success.

63: Give Detailed Responses

Fuzziness is the prelude to failure.

In project management and stakeholder communications, vague answers breed confusion, missteps, and unmet expectations. Detailed responses are essential for ensuring that everyone involved is on the same page.

Whether it's a query about timelines, budgets, or specific tasks, a thorough response ensures that everyone has the information they need to move forward confidently.

Providing detailed responses also signals to stakeholders that you are taking their concerns seriously.

A superficial answer, on the other hand, can give the impression that you are dismissive or ill-prepared, creating unnecessary friction.

64: Do Not Ignore Feedback You Do Not Want to Hear

There is nothing worse than paying for advice and then ignoring it.

Feedback—even the kind you do not want to hear—is invaluable. It can shed light on potential issues, offer fresh perspectives, and help you course-correct before small problems become major obstacles.

We tend to gravitate toward praise and validation, but ignoring constructive criticism can be a costly mistake.

Feedback from others, like colleagues, clients, or external stakeholders, can help you identify your blind spots. Often, feedback you would rather not hear is exactly what you need to consider most closely.

Disregarding the input of stakeholders signals a lack of respect for their insights. Moreover, ignored feedback often reappears later, magnified into bigger problems.

Showing that you can take critical feedback into account demonstrates humility, professionalism, and a commitment to success.

Embrace feedback, especially when it stings, as even poison can become a medicine.

65: Be Realistic

Whether it is about timelines, resources, or outcomes, grounding your assessments in reality sets the stage for a successful process.

Realism does not mean being pessimistic; it means taking a balanced approach. Consider the constraints of time, budget, manpower, and potential obstacles when making commitments.

When stakeholders are fully aware of the challenges ahead, they are more likely to remain engaged when those inevitable hurdles arise.

Be realistic about what you are willing to change and what you cannot negotiate in an adversarial situation.

If a battle has to be fought, it is better to do it quickly and on the basis of clear positions.

66: Zoom In

Nail down each macro-topic of the project, then zoom in to micro details.

Do not leave any blank space in your map or any issue unanswered.

Be as meticulous as a surgeon when you begin the operation.

Every question should have a response, every concern a solution, and every risk a mitigation plan.

It is essential to know not just the main elements of a project but also the intricacies that can determine its success or failure. Unresolved issues can unravel the entire effort.

Zooming in also allows you to anticipate problems before they arise, which is a rare skill.

Part 3: Techniques

Chapter 7:

Reasoning and Writing

67: Be Succinct and Punchy

During World War II, Winston Churchill urged his collaborators to write reports that went straight to the point and to put all the chunky contextual documents at the bottom of reports as appendices.

He won a world war by managing written communications that way. We should be able to secure (or approve) permissions for real estate projects using the same strategy.

Executive summaries and lists work like magic.

Put them at the very beginning of your report. However, write them at the end once you have analysed, digested, and laid out all the arguments in favour and against the project.

Executive summaries should be an island of clarity for the reader.

They are welcoming even in the midst of the storm of technical details that follow.

68: Be Fresh

Most people do not have time and/or patience.

Long-winded reports are repulsive.

Even if their contents are 100% correct and the arguments are very strong, they put you at a disadvantage. Together with the imaginary barrister mentioned above, always think about your end user, the reader.

Make sure that your writing is simple, straightforward, and engaging.

Familiarise yourself with Fowler's guidelines. If your report comprehensively covers all the relevant aspects of the project, there is nothing stopping you from having fun writing as well.

Put yourself in the reader's shoes.

Even if your reader disagrees completely with what you are saying, even if they tear your report apart, the sense of freshness will remain.

They will think, "*I abhor these nasty developers and their planning lackeys, but hey, I feel good when I read their documents.*"

69: Form Follows Function

Always use templates.

Avoid long planning policy sections in the main report.

Instead, put all the relevant policies in an appendix.

In the "planning policy framework" chapter of the report (or equivalent), list all the policies that you have considered.

In the "planning policy assessment" chapter, address all topics (land use, design, etc.) in order of importance. Then, "close" with a direct reference to the name/paragraph of the policy that works in your favour, demonstrating full compliance with it.

If compliance is not perfect or there is conflict, explain why the project's sum is still greater than its parts.

Ensure you thoroughly cover each topic, one by one, to ensure even the least knowledgeable reader understands that you have thoroughly explored every corner of the jungle.

70: Attack and Defend

Like in basketball, the players of the real estate game do not have the luxury of specialisation.

"Attacking" in this sense means being proactive—crafting innovative solutions, pushing boundaries, and seizing opportunities that may not be immediately obvious. This requires the willingness to advance bold arguments that push the project forward.

On the other hand, "defending" is equally important. It involves safeguarding the project against risks, countering opposing views, and being able to justify your stance.

Successful players master both skills. They know when to push and when to hold back.

Blending these two aspects effectively can lead to unexpected outcomes, making you a formidable force in any negotiation or discussion.

Just like basketball, it is about playing both ends of the court.

71: Remove Obstacles

A key part of any consultant's role is to remove obstacles that hinder progress. It does not matter if the obstacles are in your way or your counterpart's way. Try to get rid of them.

Whether you're dealing with logistical issues, conflicting stakeholder interests, or complex regulatory hurdles, your job is to clear the path to success.

Sometimes obstacles are obvious, but more often they are hidden beneath layers of information, requiring careful analysis to uncover.

Once identified, the next step is to develop strategies to remove them. This may involve negotiating with stakeholders, proposing alternative solutions. It could also mean tackling bureaucratic hurdles by engaging with regulatory bodies or finding creative ways to meet requirements without compromising on key project goals.

Removing obstacles is not just about solving immediate problems but about fostering a smooth, efficient process where momentum can be maintained. You enable the project to move forward without needless delays, guaranteeing the timely achievement of goals.

People will thank you twice for clearing the path and helping them progress at the same time.

72: Actively Use Planning Policies—Do Not Be Used by Them

Do not be passive.

The British planning system is based on discretion. The grammar of the system is made of policies, guidance, and standards, all of which can, in theory, be interpreted on a case-by-case basis.

Our job is to understand their nuances and use them proactively to shape outcomes that benefit the project.

Become an expert in the policies relevant to your project. Try to understand the intent behind them. Identify any flexibility within their language. The lame copying and pasting of text that you have not fully understood will not cut it.

Try to go at the root of any policy when necessary. Make sure that you create a dialogue between policies pulling in different directions. This is what "read as a whole" means.

This approach will allow you to craft arguments that align with the policy framework while still pushing for your project's specific needs.

Present your project as the ideal solution within the given framework, showing decision-makers how it meets or exceeds the goals of their own development plan.

73: Focus on the Site-Specific Details…

Planning decisions are not abstract theories. Rather, they are grounded in the specific circumstances of individual sites.

There is a well-known saying in common law that each case is judged on its own merits. This holds largely true in the realm of planning as well.

It is extremely important to pay attention to the distinctive characteristics of each site and the particular planning considerations that apply to it. By honing in on these details, you will be able to develop planning arguments that are more persuasive and contextually relevant.

Here, uniqueness must be mustered. Here, quirks can become into knock-out punches.

74: ...But Make the Best Use of Precedents

While every planning decision is rooted in the unique characteristics of a particular site, it is equally important to leverage precedents to strengthen your case.

Precedents can serve as powerful tools, painting a legal and planning background that has already been accepted in similar circumstances.

If a comparable site with similar challenges has been granted approval, this can signal to decision-makers that your proposal is aligned with established planning practices.

However, be mindful not to over-rely on precedents. They are a guide, not a guarantee.

Your case's strength lies in combining site-specific details with relevant past examples. Combining these two elements will give you a well-rounded argument that is grounded in both context and history.

Precedents are there to assist, not dictate.

75: Do Not Trivialise Elements That Make Your Argument Weaker

It can be tempting to downplay or gloss over elements that could weaken your position, but trivialising these aspects can quickly backfire.

Each component of your argument, whether strong or weak, contributes to the narrative.

Stakeholders, planners, and decision-makers are adept at identifying gaps or inconsistencies, and they may perceive the omission of weaknesses as a sign of dishonesty.

A more effective approach is to address weaker points head-on. Acknowledge them, offering clear, rational explanations or mitigations. This transparency demonstrates thoroughness, which reinforces your credibility.

In other words, embrace and address the weaker elements of your argument with honesty to strengthen your position. It ensures that your proposal is robust and prepared for scrutiny rather than ripe for rejection due to perceived (or actual) evasiveness.

76: Use the Planning Balance Even When It Is Not Formally Engaged

Technically speaking, the National Planning Policy Framework's "planning balance" concept does not apply to all planning applications.

In reality, all decision-makers are required to assess the pros and cons of a project against the development plan and all material considerations. This is always a balancing act.

More generally, people analyse (consciously or unconsciously) the various elements of a situation before making a judgement on it. We all have an internal balance, which is almost always switched on.

For these reasons, the most successful consultants always weigh the advantages and disadvantages of a real estate project before distilling their findings into a summary that anyone can understand.

Judges of all kinds prefer to have all the arguments laid out in front of them without discounts. They may use the balance differently and arrive at a conclusion that differs from yours, but you will have spared them the unnecessary toil of second-guessing *your* judgement.

77: Always Remain the Director of the Orchestra

When you are surrounded by maestros of their own musical instruments, there is a risk of spoiling the concert.

As a planner, it is your professional responsibility to ensure that every member of the orchestra plays in unison.

This is true for both planning consultants and planning officers.

As a planning consultant, you are the ultimate judge of the arguments to be put in front of the actual judge (planning officer, planning committee, and inspector, etc.), sometimes with the help of lawyers.

As a planning officer, you are the ultimate authority in determining the amount of weight (positive or negative) to be assigned to each aspect of a development, as well as evaluating the development as a whole against the development plan and any other relevant planning considerations.

In both situations, you must listen carefully to each orchestra member, especially the instruments without which there is no melody.

But if a violin or a trombone wants to play more than necessary or raise its volume just because it is the most important or famous instrument, be assertive, put them in the right chair, and ask them to follow the score.

Focus only on whether or not the symphony works for the public.

Chapter 8:

Professional Development

78: Learn From the Masters

Never stop reading good planning statements written by the top planning consultancies and the best local planning authorities.

Some are valuable for their conciseness, others for their organisation. Others for their depth of insight and strength of reasoning.

Keep exploring to discover new sources of inspiration.

Do not limit yourself to planning statements.

Appeal decisions for complex developments, submissions and skeleton arguments prepared by barristers, and judgements handed down by the higher courts are fantastic free resources to think better, write better, and be punchy.

Keep reading.

79: Know, Know, Know

The best way to grow (in business, in your career, in the knowledge of your industry) is to **know** the person who **knows** the things that **you** want to **know**.

Any other permutation of these three ingredients of knowledge is useless.

If you do not know anybody, you are nobody.

If you have good contacts with interesting people who do not have valuable information, they can be good friends but not business generators or mentors.

On the other hand, a quick call or a 30-minute coffee chat with a trusted person with whom you have a solid business friendship or a mentor/mentee relationship will be more fruitful than weeks spent browsing the web with the latest technological wizardry.

Make that phone call, even if it is scary. Grab that coffee, even if it is too hot.

80: Never Underestimate the Power of Continued Professional Development (CPD)

The way we do business today is vastly different from how it was done a few years ago. Still, knowledge and dependability are eternal pillars of business success.

With this in mind, CPD is not just a checkbox on a career to-do list; it is a crucial investment in your future. It encompasses a range of activities to enhance your skills, expand your knowledge, and stay current with industry trends and regulations.

Moreover, CPD signals to clients and colleagues that you are always seeking ways to better serve their needs.

By actively participating in CPD, you position yourself as a trusted expert, which can lead to new opportunities.

If CPD is not enshrined in your monthly routine, make sure your employer creates a programme for it.

Although your salary may rise over time, you are powerless to stop the steady and progressive acquisition of knowledge.

81: Keep a Tracked Program of Learning Activities

A structured approach to learning is key to achieving long-term growth.

Set clear objectives for your learning journey. Identify the knowledge areas you need to develop or refine, then choose learning activities that align with these goals, such as workshops, webinars, courses, or industry conferences.

Maintain a detailed log of these activities, including dates, topics covered, and outcomes. This helps you track your progress, assess the effectiveness of various learning methods, and stay accountable to your development plan.

By keeping a tracked programme of learning activities, you turn professional development from a vague concept into an impactful element of your career strategy.

82: Free Resources Are Usually Very Good…

We carry a small device in our pockets that can act as a portal to the sum total of all human knowledge. Most of the world gives us access to a wealth of information through various resources, many of them free. From online courses and webinars to industry blogs and professional forums, free resources offer valuable opportunities for learning without any financial commitment.

The internet is brimming with free educational content produced by experts, institutions, and organisations.

Leverage these free tools as part of a broader learning strategy to stay informed, enhance your skills, and remain competitive in your field.

PS: See **Appendix 1** for a selection of resources for town planning professionals working in the United Kingdom.

83: ...But Sometimes Spending Money Will Buy You Better Knowledge

While free resources are often excellent, there are times when paid resources can provide superior value.

Paid courses frequently offer more comprehensive content than free alternatives. Experts typically design and deliver them, offering in-depth knowledge, hands-on practice, and direct interaction with instructors, fostering a deeper understanding of complex topics.

Additionally, paid resources often include access to premium materials, such as specialised toolkits, exclusive case studies, and cutting-edge research that may not be available in free formats.

Lastly, investing in high-quality paid resources can facilitate networking opportunities with industry professionals, which can be invaluable for career advancement.

84: Build and Expand a Network of Top-Quality Professionals

Engage with these individuals to tap into their expertise, gain fresh perspectives, and stay abreast of industry trends. Their guidance can help you navigate challenges more effectively.

A strong network can also broaden your access to new opportunities. People come with their own networks and can refer you to potential clients, partners, or leads.

Building such a network requires a proactive approach. Attend industry events, participate in professional organisations, and engage in meaningful conversations with peers.

Focus on quality over quantity; a few well-established relationships with influential professionals can be more beneficial than a large number of superficial connections.

85: Include "Leftfield" Literature in the Mix

You can learn a lot from disciplines that are far away from your realm of expertise, even odd ones.

Exploring unconventional literature encourages you to approach problems from fresh perspectives.

For example, reading about behavioural economics might offer unique insights into consumer decision-making, while delving into works on cognitive science could provide new strategies for improving communication.

This cross-disciplinary approach can help you draw connections between seemingly unrelated fields, leading to novel solutions and creative approaches in your own work.

Engaging with diverse literature also broadens your intellectual horizons and stimulates curiosity. It helps you stay open-minded, which is priceless.

86: Books More Than Screens

Lo-fi paper books and documents are better than digital versions when it comes to *feeling* their message.

Scribbles at the margins are the seeds of great ideas.

The texture of the pages, the weight of the book, and even the smell of paper contribute to a deeper connection with the material.

This physical interaction enhances focus and retention, making it easier to engage with the content.

Audiobooks, too, offer a different kind of engagement, allowing you to absorb content while multitasking or on the go. However, they lack the interactive element of physical books that can stimulate active thinking and note-taking.

87: Invite Those You Admire Out for a Coffee

While most people associate networking with formal gatherings, some of the most valuable connections come from personal interactions.

When you invite a person out for coffee, you open the door to a genuine, one-on-one conversation.

The informal setting allows for a more relaxed exchange of ideas and experiences compared to the often-impersonal nature of larger networking events. It creates an opportunity for you to ask questions, seek advice, and discuss topics of mutual interest.

Your approach should reflect your admiration for them. Be specific about why you value their work and how you believe their insights could benefit you. This demonstrates your genuine respect for their work, increasing the likelihood that they will be willing to meet.

Always offer something of value in return, whether it's sharing your own experiences, offering assistance in a project, or simply being a supportive contact in their network.

88: Top Tier Professionals Are Just One LinkedIn Message Away

There is no tool more powerful than LinkedIn to create direct connections with the best of the best (clients, peers, mentees).

Its expansive network and advanced search features make LinkedIn a powerful tool for reaching out to influential figures.

Sometimes, it is the shortest path to new instructions.

When reaching out, personalise your message to demonstrate that you have done your homework and understand the key drivers of the recipient.

Highlight specific achievements or contributions that resonate with your interests. This makes your outreach stand out amidst the sea of generic connection requests.

Never talk about you but rather discuss a common ground where you can meet, either in person or virtually.

Be respectful of their time, suggesting a brief conversation or coffee chat to explore potential synergies.

It might feel daunting to reach out to someone you view as a top-tier professional, but many are open to connecting with others who show a sincere interest in their work.

Even if your initial outreach does not result in an immediate response, you have sent a signal.

Seeds can sleep for hundreds of years and still bear fruit.

Chapter 9:

Business Development

89: Be the Unique Point of Reference for Specific High-Quality Clients

Create your niche and become *the only possible choice* for clients within that niche.

It is impossible to be the *only* professional providing a certain service, but you can be the provider of an *exclusive* service for a certain group of clients.

If you love rugby, double down on rugby-orientated clients or actual rugby teams.

If your hobby is baking and you come from Venus, all Venusians with a taste for carrot cakes *must* know what your core business offering is. Why would they go to a gardening lover from Mars when they need advice on your specific area of expertise?

The possibilities are endless, as there are many passions that involve structured organisations, events, and, ultimately, the use and development of real estate.

90: Go to Events Where You Are the Only Person in the Room With Your Job Title

Professionals like to go to events where they can find colleagues to share ideas, successes, and defeats.

There is no doubt that bonding with colleagues is important. However, when you are looking for new business opportunities, it is wiser to steer clear of crowded rooms full of peers.

Rather, you should seek out environments where competition is either minimal or non-existent.

Why would you sell apples in an apple orchard? It's better to set up a shop in a town that has not seen apples for a long time.

Go to artistic events, clubs, or seminars on subjects connected to your area of expertise. Join a sports club. Go to boring events with interesting guests.

If you are an architect, go to events aimed at engineers or planners. If you are a planner, go to events where there are only architects or real estate developers around you.

In a room full of needles, try to be the only magnetic business force.

91: Don't Burn Bridges

The world is small, and it has been fully mapped. The real estate world is even smaller.

Cutting ties with colleagues, clients, or partners can have long-lasting negative effects on your professional opportunities. Try to maintain positive relationships even when situations become challenging.

The way you handle disagreements or separations speaks volumes about your professionalism. Even if you are parting ways, leave on good terms to preserve your reputation as a fair and respectful individual.

Word of your conduct can spread rapidly, and this could affect future opportunities.

To avoid burning bridges, communicate openly and professionally. Address conflicts with a problem-solving mindset and aim to resolve issues amicably. If parting ways is necessary, do so with respect and appreciation for the shared experiences and achievements.

92: Mend Bridges

While it is important to avoid burning bridges, sometimes, despite your best efforts, relationships falter. The ability to mend these bridges can turn potential setbacks into opportunities for growth.

Start by recognising the problem or conflict that led to the strain in the relationship. Avoiding the issue or pretending it does not exist will only perpetuate the problem.

Engage in honest and open dialogue. Share your thoughts while also listening to the other party's perspective. Show that you are willing to take concrete steps to rectify the situation and prevent similar issues in the future.

Rebuilding trust takes time and consistent effort, so follow through on any promises or commitments made during the reconciliation process.

Rebuilding the bridge will pay off many times over.

An "enemy" (re)turned friend can be a priceless asset.

93: Build Bridges

Building bridges is about proactively forging strong connections with colleagues, clients, and stakeholders.

Show genuine interest in their work and find common ground to build rapport.

Offer value upfront, whether through sharing insights, providing assistance, or connecting them with resources. This approach demonstrates your worth as a contact.

Look for collaborative opportunities and nurture relationships by regularly checking in.

Expanding your network through industry events and forums can also help you build bridges with a diverse range of individuals.

94: Activate Your Wider Network

Start by exploring relationships in other industries, where fresh perspectives and innovative ideas can enrich your approach. Engage with professionals who operate in fields that intersect with or complement your own.

Do not overlook individuals from unconventional backgrounds or left-field originators who may not follow the mainstream but bring creative solutions.

Their unconventional thinking can spark new ideas. Reach out to these individuals, engage in meaningful conversations, and explore potential synergies.

Additionally, activating your network includes interacting with your "best enemies," those who might be competitors, but also offer potential for strategic alliances.

95: Introduce Top Quality Professionals for Free

A lot of practitioners give away valuable work for free, such as feasibility studies, reports, or simply their time.

It is much more valuable for your clients to give away recommendations and strategic suggestions.

A feasibility study might still be a good marketing tool, but that specific project might end nowhere for many reasons outside your control or simply because your prospect has decided to use somebody else.

On the other hand, if your prospective client gets good recommendations and enriches her pool of talent thanks to you, she will remember that you are a good source of intellectual capital.

The recommendees will remember you as a source of business and will direct opportunities your way pretty soon.

Wherever possible, choose outcomes that offer this dual benefit rather than opting for a single reward that may lose its value as soon as it is received.

96: Search for Difficult and Unsexy Jobs With High Margins

Focussing on challenging tasks can offer a strategic advantage.

High-profile and glamorous projects often attract the most attention, but they can be highly competitive. Difficult and "unsexy" jobs often come with higher profit margins and less competition.

They might involve complex regulatory environments, intricate technical details, or challenging client demands.

They require a high level of expertise and persistence, which can result in substantial financial rewards. Positioning yourself to handle these demanding roles will differentiate you from others, but it will also allow you to tap into lucrative niches that others might avoid.

Tackling tough projects makes you a specialist, which can lead to further opportunities and increased respect within your industry.

97: Resolve Emergencies

Emergencies come with a mix of urgency, complexity, and high stakes.

When a crisis arises, the potential for rapid problem-solving and decisive action makes the situation more electrifying but could also lead to higher profitability.

Successfully navigating these high-pressure scenarios showcases your team's ability to manage crises effectively, turning potentially disastrous situations into triumphs.

It will also amplify your ability to thrive under pressure, which can attract more high-profile projects in the future.

Lastly, resolving crises facilitates stronger team cohesion and morale, as overcoming significant challenges together can be deeply rewarding.

98: Expand Your Pool of Prosperity

Identify potential sources of additional income that complement your current offerings.

Engage in discussions within your established networks. Bring new perspectives to the table to spark interest and generate opportunities for collaboration.

Consider building new groups or communities around emerging trends or niche interests. Positioning yourself as a leader or innovator in these new areas can help you carve out a unique market position and attract new clients or customers.

The best market is the one that already exists, but nobody has explored before.

The second best is the one you create from scratch with your own rules (see Facebook, Google, Amazon, etc.).

99: Be Trusted Above All

Trust is the only essential ingredient for success.

All the other ingredients are influenced by market conditions, location, experience, personal circumstances, and visibility.

Still, if you are good at what you do and have the trust (directly or indirectly) of your clients, someone will give you another opportunity to put your skills to work one more time.

If you are trustworthy, doors will continue to open perpetually.

The X Factor

Demolish the Walls

The demolition of real buildings will become less and less fashionable (or lawful).

However, you should be maniacal about demolishing *immediately* and *completely* any communication wall that is erected by will or by chance, affecting the spirit of collaboration with colleagues, clients, stakeholders, decision makers, and the community at large.

These walls might manifest as silos within a group, misunderstandings between teams, or even entrenched biases. Each barrier impedes the group's collective problem-solving abilities.

Encourage regular dialogue and actively work to dismantle any organisational structures or behaviours that create unnecessary divisions.

Beyond the job description in your email signature, the reality is that we are all *on the same team.*

Conclusion

When I decided to leave the public sector and join a reputable planning consultancy in the City of London, one of my Council colleagues joked that I was switching to the dark side of the force.

I politely chuckled, but I did not feel that way.

As a public planning officer, I never acted as if there was a wall dividing "us" and "them." I have always believed that working cooperatively was the only way to achieve positive outcomes for all parties involved.

Now that I advance the interests of my clients, I still strive to be positive and proactive in my communications with my counterparts in the public sector.

Thus, although this book is written from the perspective of a consultant working in the private sector, it is equally dedicated to my colleagues working in councils, public bodies, and government.

Let us demolish that communication wall together, even if we disagree on a specific project.

I hope you enjoyed reading this book.

Lorenzo

A Small Gesture

- If you found any value in this book, please recommend it to your fellow jungle explorers and share it on your social media channels.

- Do you want to share your perspective? Please write a review on Amazon; it makes a huge difference.

- Please share the good, the bad, and the ugly of your journey in the planning jungle on social media with the hashtag #HTTPJ.

Let's Work Together

Lorenzo is the founding director of Logic Planning, a boutique planning consultancy based in London specialised on residential, commercial, educational, and mixed-use developments across England.

With a blend of solid technical expertise, strategic advocacy, and commercial acumen, Logic Planning guides you through the planning system to deliver sustainable and profitable results.

Lorenzo is also a leading voice in the Italian community in the UK; he is the author of the *Real Estate a Londra* newsletter (REAL), and through his activities he has built a network of top-tier experts in the industry.

Please get in touch if:

- **You need laser-focussed planning consultancy for real estate projects in England.**
- **You want to book the CPD session *How to Thrive in the Planning Jungle* for your team.**
- **You want to discuss potential speaking opportunities with Lorenzo.**

LINKEDIN: (Lorenzo Pandolfi)

www.linkedin.com/in/lorenzo-pandolfi-72b89b88/

EMAIL:

www.info@logic-planning.com

WEBSITE:

www.logic-planning.com

Appendix 1:

Intelligence for Planning Professionals

From when I started photocopying by stealth the most famous court cases to better understand the British town planning system to my recent rather expensive purchases of obscure books on post-war master planning, I always tried to read as much as I could out of office hours.

This has helped me to learn the ABC of planning and, lately, some more advanced negotiation and people skills. During challenging times, I have found immense comfort in the excellent books that make our life easier.

It would be rude to write a text on survival techniques without acknowledging the legendary explorers of the planning jungle who have mapped it so well and make it more accessible to us every day with their razor-like insights.

This list of recommended readings and resources is certainly incomplete, but I hope it will help the younger adventurers.

I would have loved to have it on my desk when I first started out as an assistant, so I dedicate it to all the real estate professionals who, at times, feel a bit lost.

INDEX

- <u>**COMPARABLES AND CASE STUDIES**</u>
  - Planning committees' decisions (London and Home Counties)
  - Appeal decisions
  - Judicial decisions
- <u>**CRAFT**</u>
  - **Principles**
    - Ethics
    - Space awareness
    - Analysis and critical thinking
  - **Practice**
    - Advocacy
    - Writing
    - Negotiation
  - **Project management**
    - Client care and teamwork
    - Document management

        - Process management

- **COFFEE BREAK**

*   *   *

- **CONTEXT**
    - **Real estate and planning**
        - ***Real estate concepts - A handbook***, edited by Ernie Jowsey, Routledge, 2014
        - ***Urban planning and real estate development***, John Ratcliffe, Michael Stubbs, and Miles Keeping, Routledge, 2021
        - ***Property development***, Richard Reed, Routledge, 2021
        - ***Real estate investment: a strategic approach***, Andrew Baum, Routledge, 2022
    - **Who is your client?**
        - ***The real estate game***, William J. Poorvu and Jeffrey L. Cruikshank, The Free Press, 1999

- *How real estate developers think*, Peter Hendee Brown, University of Pennsylvania Press, 2015

- *Making it in real estate*, John McNellis, ULI, 2020

- *Powerhouse principles*, Jorge Pérez, Celebra, 2008

- **CORE DISCIPLINES**

  - **The planning system**

    - *Town and country planning in the UK*, Barry Cullingworth, Routledge, 2014

  - **Planning law**

    - *The essential guide to planning law*, Various Authors, Policy Press, 2017

    - *Telling & Duxbury's Planning Law and Procedure*, Oxford University Press, Latest edition

    - *A practical approach to planning law*, Ashley Bowes, Oxford University Press, Latest edition

- *An introduction to the General Permitted Development Order,* Ben Fullbrook, Law Brief Publishing, 2021

- *The essential guide to the use of land and buildings*, Martin H. Goodall, Bath Publishing, 2020

- *A practical guide to permitted changes of use*, Martin H. Goodall, Bath Publishing, 2022

- *The Planning Jungle:* www.planningjungle.com/

○ **Planning practice**

- *Encyclopaedia of planning law and practice*, Sweet & Maxwell

- *Development Control Practice (DCP) online*: www.dcp-online.co.uk/DCP

- *Planning practice: critical perspectives from the UK*, Edited by Jessica Ferm and John Tomaney, Routledge, 2018

- **CURRENT AFFAIRS**

○ **Magazines**

- *Planning Resource*: www.planningresource.co.uk
- *The Planner*: www.theplanner.co.uk
- *Local Government Lawyer*: www.localgovernmentlawyer.co.uk/planning

- **Research**
  - *Planning Matters*: (Blog) www.lichfields.uk/blog/

- **Commentary on planning decisions, planning policy and law**
  - *Simonicity*, by Simon Ricketts: (Blog) www.simonicity.com
  - *Planoraks*, by Zack Simons: (Blog) www.planoraks.com
  - *Nicola Gooch's*: (Blog) www.imbusiness.passle.net/u/102cy5l/nicola-gooch
  - *50 Shades of Planning*, by Samuel Stafford: (Blog and podcast) www.samuelstafford.blogspot.com

- ***Have We Got Planning News for You***, hosted by Chris Young KC, Mary Cook, Charlie Banner KC, Sasha White KC and Paul Tucker KC: (Live panel discussion and podcast) www.havewegotplanningnewsforyou.com

- ***The Planning Podcast***, by Richard Kimblin: (Podcast) www.open.spotify.com/show/0hQdn4I2NAJGCsRd25SoqL

- ***Planning law, unplanned***, by Simon Ricketts: (Clubhouse channel) www.clubhouse.com/house/planning-law-unplan

- **COMPARABLES AND CASE STUDIES**

  - **Planning committees' decisions (London and home counties)**

    - ***Thorncliffe London & Home Counties Planning Committee Digest***: www.thorncliffe.com/committeedigest/

    - ***London Conversations: Weekly Planning and Political Update***: www.us7.campaign-archive.com/home/?u=d6c88384a3c2f26ccd0cb3080&id=adbe12b925

- Appeal decisions
    - *COMPASS*: www.compasssearch.co.uk/CompassOnline/home
    - ***The Town Library - Planning Appeal Decisions:*** (Only major developments determined after a public inquiry) www.townlegal.com/library/planning-appeal-decisions/
- Judicial decisions
    - ***British and Irish Legal Information Institute (BAILII):*** www.bailii.org/
    - ***The Town Library - Planning Court Judgements*** (and appellate judgements): www.townlegal.com/library/planning-court-judgments/

- CRAFT
    - PRINCIPLES
        - Ethics
            - ***RTPI Code of Professional Conduct***
    - Space awareness

- ***Invisible cities***, Italo Calvino, Penguin, 2023

- ***Who plans the planning? Architecture, Politics and Mankind***, Lucius Burckhardt, Birkhauser, 2019

- ***Humanise: a maker's guide to building our world***, Thomas Heatherwick, Penguin, 2023

- **Analysis and critical thinking**

  - ***The reflective practitioner: how professionals think in action***, Donald A. Schon, Basic Books, 1984

- **PRACTICE**

  - **Advocacy**

    - ***The art of the advocate***, Richard Du Cann, Penguin, 1993

    - ***How to win every argument***, Madsen Pirie, Bloomsbury, 2017

    - ***The devil's advocate***, Iain Morley QC, Sweet & Maxwell, 2015

    - ***How to lose a case***, Edmund King QC

- Writing
  - ***Point made***, Ross Guberman, Oxford University Press, 2014
  - **Anything by Winston Churchill** (especially WWII memos)
  - **Anything by George Orwell**
  - ***Fowler's Modern English Usage***, latest edition
  - **Most reports prepared by the Trinity (DP9, Gerald Eve, Lichfields**)
- Negotiation
  - ***Essential negotiation***, Gavin Kennedy, The Economist, 2004
  - ***Yes! - 60 secrets from the science of persuasion***, Noah Goldstein, Steve Martin and Robert Cialdini, Profile Books, 2017
  - ***Never split the difference***, Chris Voss, Harper Business, 2016

- **PROJECT MANAGEMENT**
  - **Client care and teamwork**

- ***Secrets to optimal client service***, Jim Donovan, University of Virginia School of Law: www.youtube.com/watch?v=hJbwyN4ZoCg

- ***Conflict in construction: avoiding, managing, resolving***, Jeffery Whitfield, Wiley-Blackwell, 2012

- ***How to win friends and influence people***, Dale Carnegie, Vermilion, 2006

▪ **Document management**

- ***Sedley's Laws of Documents***

▪ **Process management**

- ***Process! How Discipline and Consistency Will Set You and Your Business Free***, Mike Paton and Lisa González, Benbella, 2022

- ***The 80/20 Principle: Achieve More with Less***, Richard Koch, Nicholas Brealey Publishing, 2022

- **COFFEE BREAK**

  ○ ***Grotton Revisited***, Steve Ankers, David Kaiserman and Chris Shepley, Routledge, 2010

- ***Epic Space: The Architectural Diaries***, Ian Martin, 2017
- ***Forensic Fables by O***, (Wildy Classics) by Theo Mathew, Wildy, Simmonds & Hill, 2013
- ***The Dilbert Principle***, Scott Adams, Boxtree, 2000

Printed in Dunstable, United Kingdom

74702047R10080